My Canadian Family

Brush Your Teeth

Written and Illustrated by Laura Lee Fedoryshin Prashad

This book is for my girls whose smiles can make any moment special.

2024 My Canadian Family Paperback Edition

My Canadian Family is an Imprint of Lyanraura Inc.

Copyright © 2024 Laura Lee Fedoryshin Prashad. Illustrations copyright © 2024 Laura Lee Fedoryshin Prashad. Initial illustrations for character design of "Mom" were contributed by Kenneth Togonon. All rights reserved. No part of this book may be reproduced or transmitted in any form or by any means, electronic or mechanical, including photocopying, recording, or by any information storage and retrieval system, without written permission from the author. For information address Laura@mycanadianfamily.ca

Printed in Canada

ISBN Softcover 978-1-0688862-3-2

ISBN Hardcover 978-1-0688862-5-6

ISBN Ebook 978-1-0688862-4-9

Brushing teeth stops tooth decay
That's why we brush them twice a day!

 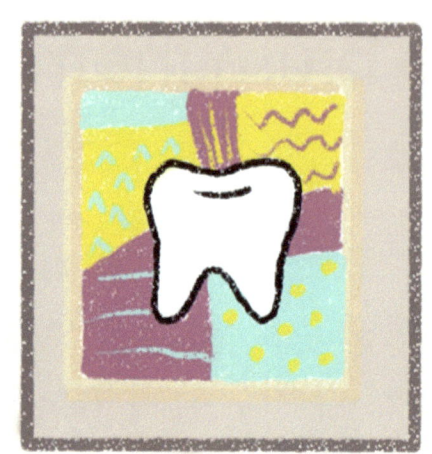 

I'll show you how to do it right!
When you brush morning and night

First we need to rinse the brush

Then add some **toothpaste** but not too much

Brush in a circle on those **incisors**
They're shiny now and you look wiser!

Incisors are used for biting. Their name originates from the Latin word 'incidere', which means 'to cut'

Now round and round on those **canines**
Keep on going, make them shine!

Canines rip and tear food and are named for their resemblance to dog teeth. Canines come to a single, pointy cusp which is why they are also called cuspids.

Reach to the right and at the back
Brush away all the **plaque**

Plaque is made of bacteria, little bits of food and saliva. Bacteria acids in plaque eat away at tooth enamel, which can cause cavities and gum disease

To the back and left now please, Say no thanks to **cavities**.

Cavities are holes in your teeth. Untreated cavities can lead to illness and pain as well as trouble eating and speaking.

Very good now **open wide**
Make sure that you brush
inside

Brush,
Brush,
Brush
the **top**.

Then the **bottoms**, don't you stop!

Brush the inside of the molars too

Molars are your biggest teeth. They have a they have 5-6 cuspids (points) so they can chew food and grind it up.

Keep it up you're almost through!

At last, all of the teeth are done, So it's time to brush your **tongue**!

Brushing your tongue can help reduce bad breath! Be careful not to brush too hard you don't want to break the skin.

Ask for a little help before you are through

And open wide for a moment or two.

Spit out any extra toothpaste now,
Look at your smile
So **shiny**! Wow!

To keep the toothpaste on the teeth longer and prevent cavities spitting, not rinsing is recommended

Tips for a Better Brushing Experience

1. <u>Keep it quick</u>
   Until your little one is comfortable brushing aim for "small wins" you don't need to spend 2 minutes right away.
   Here is a great starting place:
   Ask the child to say Ahhh and brush the inside
   Ask the child to say Eeee and brush incisors and canines
   The first time you do it spend 2 seconds on each spot then increase the time as they become more comfortable

2. <u>Be Patient</u>
   "We need to brush your teeth but I will wait until you are ready"

3. <u>Practice Outside of the Bathroom</u>
   Incorporate brushing teeth into your play. You can use dolls, model teeth or dinosaurs.

4. <u>Be Positive</u>
   It's ok to use too much toothpaste
   It's ok if we take too long
   Celebrate trying

If you enjoyed this book, it would mean the world if you could take a moment to leave a heartfelt review on Amazon. Your feedback is deeply appreciated and incredibly valuable. Thank you sincerely for your time

www.ingramcontent.com/pod-product-compliance
Lightning Source LLC
Chambersburg PA
CBHW041437010526
44118CB00002B/99